THE CLAN M A ͡

(CL

THE J

BY

W. R. KERMACK

Author of *Here's Scotland's Story*, *The Scottish Highlands*,
The Scottish Borders

The cover shows the MacGregor tartan and the clansmen's
cap or sash badge.

Clansman's Badge

JOHNSTON & BACON PUBLISHERS
EDINBURGH AND LONDON

FIRST PUBLISHED 1953
SECOND EDITION 1963
REPRINTED 1969
REPRINTED 1972
THIRD EDITION 1979
Reprinted 1993
© *1993 Johnston & Bacon (Books) Ltd.*
ISBN 0 7179 4266 X

Printed in Scotland by PRINTALL, Gartocharn G83 8RY

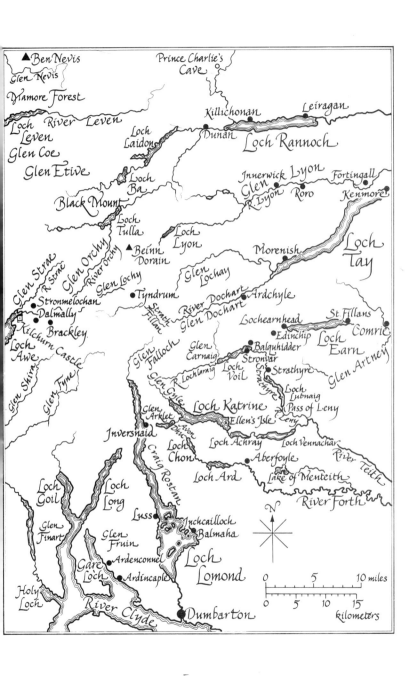

Genealogies of the House of Glenorchy

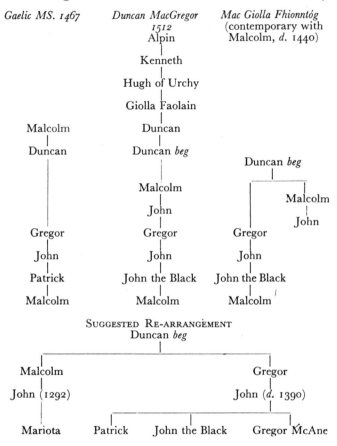

Gaelic MS. 1467	Duncan MacGregor 1512	Mac Giolla Fhionntóg (contemporary with Malcolm, d. 1440)
	Alpin	
	Kenneth	
	Hugh of Urchy	
	Giolla Faolain	
Malcolm	Duncan	
Duncan	Duncan *beg*	
		Duncan *beg*
	Malcolm	Malcolm
	John	John
Gregor	Gregor	Gregor
John	John	John
Patrick	John the Black	John the Black
Malcolm	Malcolm	Malcolm

SUGGESTED RE-ARRANGEMENT

Duncan *beg*

Malcolm — Gregor

John (1292) — John (*d.* 1390)

Mariota — Patrick — John the Black — Gregor McAne

Glenorchy

WEST of Tyndrum (" the house of the ridge ") the main route between Argyll and Perthshire crosses the water-shed that divides the western from the eastern Highlands. East of the water-shed is Strathfillan, the upper part of Glendochart. West of the water-shed the Lochy flows to join the Orchy, of which the Water of Tulla is the head-stream, while a mile below Bridge of Orchy the Allt Chonoghlais comes in from the back of Beinn Dorain. By the Allt Chonoghlais there is access to the long glen of the Lyon in Perthshire. The Strae, its last tributary, joins the Orchy just before the river enters Loch Awe. It seems logical to identify the Orchy, the Strae, and the Lochy as the MacGregors' " three glens," though Glen-lyon and Glendochart also have been suggested. The best land was the Strath of Orchy below its junction with the Lochy ; Glenstrae is narrow and only eight miles long. The hill country, however, was a fit hunting-ground for kings.

At Fortingall on the Lyon, Tulaich a' Mhuilinn was occupied at the beginning of the sixteenth century by two MacGregor brothers, whose ancestor about a hundred years earlier had managed to procure for himself and his heirs the vicarage of Fortingall and a lease of the church lands. The elder brother, James, was Vicar of Fortingall and Dean of Lismore in Argyll. To him and to his brother Duncan was due the collection of the mass of Gaelic verse preserved in the *Book of the Dean of Lismore*. This fortunately includes the compositions of five bards in praise of MacGregor chiefs, which supplement our scanty information on the early history of the clan.

The name " Clan Gregor " means " the children of

Gregor," but the earliest kinsfolk of the clan of whom
we have knowledge did not use this name. They took
their style from their territory. From the Act of Parliament
by which in 1292 King John Baliol formed a sheriffdom
of Argyll, we find that sheriffdom included the lands of
a certain John of Glenorchy. In 1296 he was made
prisoner by the English at Dunbar, and did homage to
Edward I of England, when his lands were apparently
restored to him on the condition of fighting for Edward
in France. In the *Book of the Dean of Lismore* there is a
genealogy of Clan Gregor in which John Eoin is the name
of the father of the only Gregor mentioned. It
seems an inevitable conclusion that, from this Gregor,
Clan Gregor took their name, for it is hardly to be
imagined that a genealogy of the clan would omit the
individual after whom the clan were named ; and John
of Glenorchy of 1292 might be identified as his father.
There is reason, however, to doubt whether this can be
accepted. In the Dean's genealogy Gregor is the son of
John, son of Malcolm, son of Duncan *beg* (" the little ").
But a poem by the bard Mac Giolla Fhionntóg in the
Dean's Book refers to Duncan *beg* as the father of Gregor
as well as of Malcolm ; while in another Clan Gregor
genealogy, included in a Gaelic manuscript of 1467,
Gregor is shown as the son of Duncan, son of Malcolm.
These sources of evidence, both earlier than the Dean's
genealogy, thus agree that Gregor's father was Duncan,
who was father of Malcolm except in the 1467 genealogy
where the name of Duncan's son *may* in error have been
given to Duncan's father. Malcolm is surely to be
identified as the father of John who possessed Glenorchy ;
Malcolm was therefore presumably older—it is likely,
much older—than Gregor, if Gregor was his brother or
half-brother, in which case Gregor's descendants were a
junior branch of the house of Glenorchy.

From Duncan *beg* the Dean's genealogy carries the ancestry of Clan Gregor three generations back to Hugh of Urchy, in Gaelic *Aodh Urchaidh* ; and the name of Hugh's son, Giolla Faolain, " the servant of St. Fillan," points to a connection with the neighbouring Celtic monastery of St. Fillan in Glendochart. The abbot of Glendochart, in the Law called Claremathan about the beginning of the thirteenth century, takes part on the same footing as the Earl of Atholl in the administration of justice in Central Argyll, and thus in Glenorchy. Hugh of Urchy may then have been a native ruler in Argyll in this way brought into contact with the abbey, or he may have become established in Glenorchy through a connection with the family of the abbot. The Macnabs —*Clann an Aba*, " children of the abbot "—probably descend from an abbot of Glendochart ; and Malcolm and Patrick of Glendochart, who were evidently laymen holding lands in Glendochart, submitted, like John of Glenorchy, to Edward in 1296. " Glenorchy " apparently comprised also Glen Lochy and Glenstrae.

When John of Glenorchy's lands were specifically included in the sheriffdom of Argyll, he must have held them directly from the king. His line apparently ended in an heiress (daughter or granddaughter), Mariota de Glenurquhay, to whom, and to her husband John Campbell (considered by *The Scots Peerage* probably to have been the son of Sir Colin Campbell of Lochawe), Glenorchy was granted by royal charter in 1357. It is possible that the Glenorchy family had already lost the position of tenants-in-chief of the Crown, if Glenorchy was included in the barony of Lochawe, of which Robert Bruce gave a charter in 1315 to Sir Colin Campbell, John Campbell's father. In that case Glenorchy would have been taken out of the barony in order to provide for John Campbell and his bride, who may have been the

ward of Lochawe. Even so, from the precedence given
to Mariota in the grant, she seems likely to have been
the heiress of Glenorchy. John Campbell and Mariota's
line evidently failed, presumably from lack of an heir ;
when either Gregor or (more probably) his son must have
come into Glenorchy as the heir male of the original
Glenorchy family, since the death of John of Glenorchy,
son of Gregor, is recorded in 1390. This seems additional
evidence that, even if Gregor *was* a son of John of Glenorchy (1292), he was a younger son, and his line was
junior to that represented by Mariota. Gregor's family
would call themselves MacGregors after their founder.
Moreover, for several generations from Hugh of Urchy,
branches of his house had doubtless received tacks or
leases in the " three glens." They would look on the
contemporary head of Hugh's house as the chief of their
clan ; and they too, when Gregor's line became the
principal family, may have taken the surname MacGregor.

It is probable, however, that the house of Glenorchy
had now irrevocably lost their position as tenants-in-chief
of the Crown ; that after John Campbell's death the
Campbells continued to claim superiority over Glenorchy ; and that neither Gregor nor his descendants
ever held Glenorchy except as tenants of Lochawe, thus
marking the first step in the eventual shattering of Clan
Gregor. At any rate, in 1432, Sir Duncan Campbell of
Lochawe was in a position to grant his property lands
of Glenorchy to his son Colin, who became the first
Campbell Laird of Glenorchy under this new grant, and
confirmed his hold by building the castle of Kilchurn on
Loch Awe. For this final loss by the MacGregors of
Glenorchy, so long the home of their race, the way must
presumably have been cleared by the death of a Mac-
Gregor tenant of Glenorchy who left no direct male heir.
The 1467 genealogy gives John of Glenorchy (the son of

Gregor) an eldest son, Patrick. He or a son Malcolm may have died in 1432 leaving no heir. Glenstrae, indeed, was not included in the grant of Glenorchy to Colin Campbell. It continued to be held by Malcolm, son of John the Black, son of John of Glenorchy. Malcolm succeeded to the chiefship, and he, his son Patrick, and Patrick's son, a second John the Black, occupied Glenstrae as tenants of Lochawe. Similarly the descendants of Gregor McAne, a third son of John of Glenorchy, held Brackley of Lochawe as superior. But this final loss of Glenorchy was crippling. It compelled MacGregors, for whom there was no room in the meagre clan territory, to live outside it, dispersed under alien landlords. This event was the second and decisive factor which brought about the downfall of the clan.

At this crisis of their fortune, the clan were heartened by an assurance that their ancestry was royal. The genealogy in the Dean's Book, by Duncan, brother of the Dean, is stated to have been written in 1512, and to have been taken " from the books of the genealogies of the kings." It traces the descent of his chief, through Hugh of Urchy, from Alpin, the father of Kenneth, " High King of Scotland," Hugh being recorded as Kenneth's son. Certainly belief in descent from Alpin became a conviction ; the clan used the motto, " Royal is my Race," 'S Rioghal Mo Dhream. At some point, however, it was realised that three hundred years must have separated King Kenneth from Hugh of Urchy ; and then Gregor, said to have been the third son of Alpin, was substituted for Kenneth as the clan's ancestor and for the genealogies' Gregor as the source of their Name. This claim to descent from Alpin led to the formation of Bonds of Friendship between MacGregor chiefs and chiefs of other clans who had traditions of the same ancestry. In 1591 Alasdair MacGregor of Glenstrae

and Aulay Macaulay of Ardincaple, "understanding
ourselfs and our name to be M'Calppins of auld and to
be our just and trew surname whereof we are all cumin,"
bind themselves to aid each other against all persons,
excepting only the king. In 1671 James MacGregor of
MacGregor and Lauchlan Mackinnon of Strathardill in
Skye bound themselves similarly as being " descended
lawfully frae twa brethren of auld descent." This tradition
of Alpin as a common ancestor, held also by a number
of other clans, is paralleled by the attribution of the
Scots fir as a badge to all those clans. In the Gaelic
lament for MacGregor of Roro, perhaps as early as about
1603, there is an allusion to this as the MacGregor
emblem. A " sword and fir-tree crossit beneath ane
croun " are mentioned in a bitter verse, " Of the Mac-
Gregor's Arms," written into a book belonging to Black
Duncan, Laird of Glenorchy 1583–1631, and appear also
in the arms of " Macgregoyre " in an English MS. of
1589. On the other hand, in an earlier Scottish MS.
(c. 1565–66) and in the modern arms the place of the
fir-tree is taken by an oak, perhaps to distinguish the
MacGregor arms from the general " Clan Alpin " badge.

Glenstrae

AFTER their loss of Glenorchy the MacGregor chiefs lived
at Stronmelochan at the foot of Glenstrae. Their burial
place was in Glenorchy at Dysart (*Diseart Chonndin—*
Connán's Hermitage), Dalmally. The poems in the
Dean's Book show them defiantly claiming their ancestors'
possessions. John the Black, Malcolm's grandson, is still
" white-toothed falcon of the three glens," and " chief of
Glenlyon." To Malcolm " the hunting of Scotland
belongs " ; while John the Black is " the king at lifting

cattle." Clan Gregor " show no fear, even when with the king they strive." This was dangerous doctrine.

John the Black left no heir, but Lochawe (now Earl of Argyll) accepted as his tenant in Glenstrae another

THE HOUSE OF GLENSTRAE

(According to A. G. Murray MacGregor, *History of the Clan Gregor*)

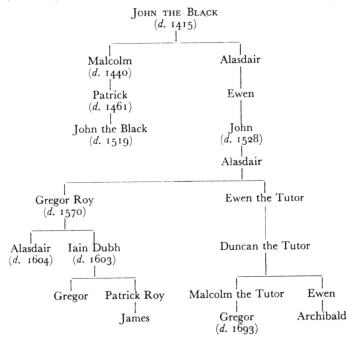

John MacGregor, presumably because he had married a Campbell. The whole clan may not at once have taken him as chief. Miss Murray MacGregor, in her *History of the Clan Gregor*, holds him to have been John the Black's second cousin. The contemporary *Black Book of Taymouth*, however, says that he was " not righteous air to the McGregour," but was " principal " of the branch of Clan Gregor called Clan Dougal Ciar (" dusky ") after its founder, whose name only is known. At the end of the century there were considered to be three " houses," or branches, referred to, probably contemptuously, by Sir Alexander Hay, Clerk of the Privy Council, as (1) " the laird's ain gang " (i.e., Glenstrae) ; (2) " the gang and hous of Roro," in Glenlyon ; and (3) " the hous and gang of Gregor McAne." This Gregor (who died in 1415) was a son of John (Eoin) of Glenorchy, and a (younger?) brother of the earlier John the Black. The author of the *History of the Clan Gregor* holds that one of his sons was the founder of the House of Roro, another was Dougal Ciar, and another, John, senior to both, got Brackley in Glenorchy. John's descendants were " the hous of Gregor McAne," to the senior line of which belonged Duncan Ladasach, of whom hereafter. A junior line succeeded to Brackley ; members were Keepers of Kilchurn castle for the Campbells of Glenorchy during strife with Glenstrae. If, however, John, who obtained Glenstrae in 1519, was " principal " of the Clan Dougal Ciar, disinheritance of the " righteous air " endangered the chiefs' hold over the clan: this also contributed to their downfall.

Members of all these branches were scattered widely, wherever they could find holdings. For, just as the Campbells' acquisition of Glenorchy facilitated their expansion eastwards into Breadalbane, so the Mac-Gregors' loss of Glenorchy, in 1357 and again in 1432, probably enforced an eastward dispersion of Clan Gregor. The original family of Glenorchy, their ancestors, may have had lands in Perthshire by connection with the abbey of Glendochart. MacGregors may have been in Glenlyon, perhaps, for instance, as royal officials or Crown tenants in the Toiseachd of Roro (a stretch of about four miles on the south bank of the river excluded from the Barony of Glenlyon) before it was granted to Menzies of Weem early in the fifteenth century. But there is little actual evidence that MacGregors were extensively settled outside Argyll before their loss of Glenorchy, the family of the Vicar of Fortingall at Tulaich a' Mhuilinn being obviously an exceptional case. A John MacGregor was Lord of Ardenconnel in Dunbartonshire in 1429 ; but the first mentions of MacGregors in Glenlyon are at " Coreheynan " (if that is Coire Eoghanan in upper Glenlyon) in 1468 and the death of Duncan Beg at Roro in 1477. Duncan's descendants were in Roro, apparently as tenants of Menzies, for nearly three hundred years. By 1504 a MacGregor was at Innerwick on the north bank of the Lyon ; and, probably from Glenlyon, Mac-Gregors spread eastwards into the Dale of Fortingall as tenants of its successive proprietors, and, under similar conditions, to Loch Tay. They seem to have been at Balloch (Taymouth) by 1491, and at Morenish by 1503 ; but from Balloch they were ejected by Campbell of Glenorchy in 1552.

The dispersal of Highland clansmen under alien landlords was fairly common at this time, and became more common later. Unfortunately for Clan Gregor, their clansmen thus dispersed soon came to comprise by far the majority of the clan. To the alien landlord his MacGregor tenants paid their rents ; but their allegiance was still to Glenstrae, the chief of their own Name. To him their " calp " had been given, i.e., the promised payment at their death of their best beast. It was the alien landlord, however, who by law was answerable for these tenants, of whose services in " hosting (war) and hunting " he was thus deprived. With mutual restraint this position was tolerable ; but if the alien landlord turned out his MacGregor tenants, they lost their means of honest living, and their chief became responsible for clansmen who must henceforth be landless " broken men." The only solution, if eviction was to be avoided, was that MacGregors under an alien landlord should give to him their calps and bonds of manrent, or service, and renounce their allegiance to Glenstrae. This the clan were certain to oppose ; but it became increasingly difficult for the chief to control his dispersed clansmen, the difficulty naturally being greater the farther they were from Glenstrae. The only alternative to his desertion of his people in a crisis, perhaps of their own creation, was apt to be his acceptance of full responsibility for their actions by placing himself at their head.

Serious trouble seems to have arisen first in Rannoch ; for in this wild and remote glen also MacGregors had settled, coming, it is thought, north from Glenlyon. There Duncan called Ladasach (" lordly ")—from whose estate of Ardchoille (" height of the wood " or " high wood "), now Ardchyle in Glendochart, the MacGregors' war cry is held to be derived—had made himself leader of the wilder spirits, and, with a long career of lawlessness behind him, kept Perthshire far and wide in fear. In a luckless hour for Clan Gregor his reputation and his seniority [1] enabled him, during a young chief's minority, to assume the leadership of the clan, and when that chief, Alasdair, came of age, to bring him under his influence. It was at this period that, in the words of a modern biographer, Clan Gregor " acquired the evil reputation that dogged their steps and thwarted every attempt to save them." Menzies, the king's bailie for the Crown lands north of Loch Rannoch, protested his inability to keep order (1523) ; and it was probably in his stead

[1] Moncreiffe (*Highland Clans*) says Ladasach (a descendant of Gregor McAne) represented the line kept out of Glenstrae; he was probably the rightful chief. Their activities kept embroiling the clan with the Government.

that Atholl and Robertson of Struan subsequently
"policed" Rannoch. In turn Alasdair and Duncan
Ladasach in 1545 burned Struan's house at Trochry in
Strath Bran, and carried off Struan himself. Ladasach
also fell upon the MacLarens. When Alasdair died,
Duncan Ladasach became Tutor of his heir.

In Breadalbane a dozen or so MacGregor families by
the middle of the sixteenth century were settled near
Loch Tay ; and in Breadalbane the Campbells of Glenorchy had now become supreme, a cadet branch being
in Glenlyon. For a time they remained content with
rents from their MacGregor tenants. Grey Colin, the
sixth Laird, however, converted into feudal tenures leases
formerly held from the Church or from the Crown, and
naturally required of his tenants not only rents but
military service. He set about obtaining the dependence
of individual MacGregors, and in 1550 took a bond of
manrent from the tenant of Morenish, Alasdair called
Odhar ("pale"). By Alasdair's defection the integrity
of the clan probably seemed threatened ; he was murdered
by Duncan Ladasach, perhaps in his capacity as Tutor
of Glenstrae. Grey Colin, however, caught and executed
Ladasach ; and within six months nine MacGregor
families gave him their bonds of manrent. This may
well have convinced Grey Colin that what stood between
him and the service of his MacGregor tenants was the
proximity of a MacGregor chief. At any rate he bought
from Argyll his superiority over Glenstrae, and in 1560
refused to accept Gregor Roy, the son of Alasdair, as his
tenant when the young chief came of age.

Only their possession of Glenstrae now gave the
MacGregor chiefs a status better than that of leaders of
"broken men." At once the clan revolted, Glenorchy's
MacGregor tenants in Breadalbane renouncing their
bonds of manrent to him. For ten years Gregor Roy

carried on a private war with Grey Colin, in the course of which Glenorchy, as deputy for Menzies, brought in Camerons and Macdonalds of Keppoch to clear the MacGregors from Rannoch. These, however, were unlikely to prove satisfactory tenants ; Menzies complained to the Queen, and was authorised to reinstate the MacGregors. But in his probable main object Grey Colin was successful. Driven to ever more desperate actions, Gregor Roy was outlawed, and in the end was captured and beheaded at Kenmore. His widow, Marion, a daughter of Glenlyon, mourned her beloved in terms to us strangely primitive : " They poured his blood on the ground ; oh ! had I a cup I would drink of it my fill " ; while his clan laid waste the glen of the Orchy to the castle of Kilchurn.

In spite, or because of this, Grey Colin did not molest Glenstrae ; and Gregor's boys grew to manhood at Stronmelochan in years of respite secured by their uncle Ewen's success, as Tutor, in obtaining the patronage of Campbell of Calder, a cadet of Argyll. The young chief, Alasdair, became a noted hunter and archer, and won for himself the bye-name of the *Arrow of Glenlyon*. From Dr. A. A. W. Ramsay's biography under that title it is clear that his sense of duty to his clansmen, and his determination never to fail them, led both chief and clan to disaster in the end. He applied, when he came of age in 1588, to be invested in Glenstrae. As his father was refused by Grey Colin, so was he refused by Black Duncan, the new Laird of Glenorchy. Unlike his father, he appealed to the sheriff court ; but by Glenorchy's personal opposition, the proceedings were stopped. Alasdair could only consider himself cheated of his heritage. Bitterly resentful, he was presently called to make an instant decision in a crisis due to the action of MacGregors remote from his control. This time the trouble did not affect Rannoch or Breadalbane in Central Perthshire. It was perilously near the Lowland border, coming from the glens between Ben More and Ben Lomond that were the home of Clan Dougal Ciar.

It is rather surprising to find this branch of Clan Gregor in Balquhidder, Glengyle, and the valley of the Avondhu, a head-stream of the Forth, and in nearby Glen Arklet, stretching westwards to Loch Lomond. Even the abbots of Glendochart could hardly have established the clan's ancestors so far south of Glendochart ; and no bard in the *Book of the Dean of Lismore* claims this territory for the MacGregor chiefs. Their presence is most likely to have been the result of migration, perhaps by Glen Falloch, since it was the western portions of the three main glens that they occupied. The feudal superiors of those three glens, from south to north, were the Earl of Menteith, the Laird of Buchanan, and Murray of Tullibardine. It is as tenants of Menteith on Loch Ard and Loch Chon in the Avondhu valley that MacGregors are first mentioned in this region in 1499–1500 ; and it is in connection with trouble in 1533 between the Earl and Malcolm MacGregor " McCoule Kere " that Clan Dougal Ciar are first specifically linked with this neighbourhood. Twelve years later Duncan " McCoulekerry " of Corrarklet took part in an attack on troops of the Regent Arran, then engaged in a siege of Dumbarton. Such a proximity to important Lowland centres gave the activities of Clan Dougal Ciar a dangerous notoriety. In 1574 they are mentioned in Balquhidder. By 1581 Gregor Dubh, a son of Malcolm " McCoule Kere," was in Glengyle ; if he did not actually owe his tenancy to his marriage with a Buchanan, it must have confirmed his position. Five years later his brother, Patrick Roy, is known to have been in Strathyre.

It was not Clan Dougal Ciar who in 1589 murdered

the King's forester, Drummond of Drummond-Ernoch, in Glenartney. This seems to have been a chance act of MacGregor vengeance for kinsmen hanged for poaching deer, carried out by some of Ladasach's descendants known as MacEagh—Children of the Mist. But it was to Balquhidder that the murderers fled ; at Balquhidder Kirk that Alasdair mustered the clan, laid his hand upon the dead man's severed head, and took upon himself the blood-guilt, as did they all. This was a desperate course. An Act of 1581 had authorised reprisals, even death, against any member of an offender's clan in the offender's stead. Parliament's " General Band " of 1587 bound a chief to find hostages for the fulfilment of his obligation to surrender guilty clansmen, which failing, he was to be " persewit with fire and sword." But Alasdair had no real choice. Drummond-Ernoch was Clan Gregor's enemy ; and even if the chief had wished to hand the murderers over to justice, the clan would hardly have allowed this. For such an act a chief of Keppoch was deposed.

Though outlawed and condemned to death, Clan Gregor survived. Fiercely they defended themselves. " Chief of Stronmelochan, child of the king ! Like the storm was thy face in the field." The Government, moreover, having no military force of its own, had to entrust the execution of its decrees to local great land-owners. This Glenorchy and the kinsfolk of the murdered man alone undertook, to the extent of entering neigh-bours' territories in arms—a procedure to which they naturally objected. The outlaws were sheltered not only by Atholl and Menzies, but through Calder's influence even in Argyll. It was Calder, too, who eventually obtained for Alasdair and his people a pardon for their crime. Their escape was a narrow one, for a month later Calder was murdered.

Clan Gregor could expect no second chance. Their

name headed a list of "wickit thevis and lymmaris (blackguards) of the clannis." As the "General Band" began to be enforced, landlords got rid of their liability for MacGregor tenants by evicting them ; Menzies tried to evict Alasdair himself from an estate in Rannoch. Yet Alasdair was responsible for all these landless clansmen, whom local landlords found it dangerously convenient to employ in feuds against their neighbours. For ten years he managed so to hold them that Clan Gregor were charged with no bloodshed, though every bad winter threatened many of them with starvation. He sought no more than legal redress when Macleans harried his people in Rannoch ; and for a time he contrived to find hostages for his control of his clan.

For his final failure of control, in his "Confession" at his trial, Alasdair blamed Archibald, Earl of Argyll. We have only Glenstrae's side of the story. No legal charge was ever made for MacCailein Mór to answer ; and indeed, had such been made, he could, as Justice-General of Scotland, have been judge as well as accused. We know that Alasdair failed to replace his hostages, which caused the Privy Council to hand complete control of Clan Gregor over to Argyll. Alasdair surrendered to him, Black Duncan taking the opportunity to burn Stronmelochan, and to evict the MacGregors from Glenstrae. Alasdair says that he resisted demands that he should attack several individuals obnoxious to Argyll ; that Argyll then encouraged Iain Dubh, Alasdair's brother, and his cousins "to commit baith hership (plunder) and slauchter upone the Laird of Luss" (Colquhoun) ; and that, his kinsfolk being thus committed, he himself yielded to the Earl's promises and threats. Iain Dubh, who lived at Stronvar in Balquhidder, was certainly as conveniently placed for Argyll's alleged purpose as he was remote from his brother's control.

At any rate, whether under pressure from Argyll or to identify himself with his clan, Alasdair raided the Lennox, though without bloodshed. In a foray led by Duncan, his cousin, however, Colquhouns were wounded and killed, whereupon King James VI authorised Luss to proceed against Clan Gregor. Alasdair did not wait to be harried. Coming south from Rannoch he mustered three hundred men, including some Camerons and Mac-Ians of Glencoe ; Luss, with Colquhouns, Buchanans, and burgesses of Dumbarton, had more than their strength. But when, in February 1603, the two forces met in Glen Fruin, the MacGregors broke their foes with heavy slaughter, and swept Colquhoun's country bare. Clan Gregor lost one man of note only—Iain Dubh. Yet their victory was fatal. Gained, twelve miles from Dumbarton castle, over an opponent commissioned by the King, it was an intolerable insult to the Crown. The victors' reputation was against them, and the Government determined to make an end. " That unhappie and detestable race " was to be " extirpat and ruttit out." Their name was to be known no more in Scotland, under the penalty of death. Innocent MacGregors had to take other names ; but the victors of Glen Fruin were outlaws, whom anyone could capture or kill, and be rewarded with all their possessions.

For almost a year the chief evaded capture, until the night when he parted from his people—" Dark was the glen, and long the farewell "—and gave himself up to Argyll, on the Earl's promise (according to Alasdair's " Confession ") to " saif my lyfe and landis." At any rate Argyll evidently guaranteed his safe-conduct into England, where he intended to seek pardon from the King ; for into England he was indeed taken. But he was immediately brought back to the capital, to stand his trial before a jury that included a number of his bitterest foes. By his accusation against Argyll he hoped to obtain a sentence only of exile for himself and his clansmen ; but his " Confession " was used to prove his guilt of the slaughter at Glen Fruin and the plundering of Luss, and thereby of treason. On 20th January, 1604, he was hanged at the Mercat Cross of Edinburgh, together with eleven others of his clan. " Luckless was thy foray, Son of Red Gregor ! "

Landless

THE Gaelic poem called " MacGregor of Roro " is a lament for a MacGregor who perished after Glen Fruin. It is also a warning to the living, outlawed and hunted.

Make winter as autumn, the wolf-days as summer ;
Thy bed be the bare rock, and light be thy slumber.

Not only those suffered who had been in arms at Glen Fruin. Before he gave himself up, Alasdair had seen the consequences of the Government's policy, which he described in his " Confession " :—" to putt down innosent men, to cause pure bairnes and inffantis bege, and pure wemen to perisch for hunger, quhen they ar heirit (plundered) of thair geir." Of course these were results of his own action also ; but this did not acquit the Government of responsibility. They sought to restore order by measures (admittedly such as would have been used in any other country at that time) which were bound to entail innocent misery.

Under pain of death all men of the Name of MacGregor had to take another surname (April, 1603). Ten years later death was pronounced against members of the clan if more than four of them met together. In 1621 those who still kept the Name became doubly liable to the extreme penalty if they possessed any weapon other than a pointless knife to cut their meat. Since nobody could be expected to do the Government's work without recompense, anyone who captured a guilty MacGregor or produced his head was rewarded either with the MacGregor's possessions or with a payment of blood-money, MacGregors being invited to win a pardon for their own offences by slaughtering fellow clansmen. Women of the clan who failed to take another name were to be branded on the face and thereafter transported. Children had to change their names ; and it was intended that those over twelve years of age should be shipped to Ireland, younger children being sent to the Lowlands until they reached the age of twelve. Persons, however, who had become sureties for MacGregor parents protested that they could not be responsible for the parents' conduct if their innocent children were so treated ; and ultimately the MacGregor " bairns " were put in the charge of local landowners. Severe penalties, including fines up to the loss of all the offender's possessions, were to be inflicted on those who " reset " guilty MacGregors, that is, who sheltered or helped them in any way.

The Government's declared purpose to destroy the clan resulted in a surprisingly small number of actual executions. Probably few MacGregors were taken alive. Between 20th May 1603 and 2nd March 1604 thirty-six only were brought to trial. Nearly all of these were condemned to death ; and in addition six hostages in the Government's hands seem to have been hanged without a trial. Many more men and women of all ranks and ages, and of all branches of the clan, must have perished at the hands of their enemies or of privation and hunger. Sons of Ewen the Tutor, of Ladasach, and of Brackley, and the Roro chieftain, died by the rope or by the sword, as did other leading MacGregors.

Nevertheless Duncan, the late chief's cousin, acting as Tutor of Glenstrae for Alasdair's nephew—Iain Dubh's eldest boy—the heir to the chiefship, could still bring out six or seven score desperate men when in 1611 King James ordered Argyll, as his Royal Lieutenant, " by justice and the swerd to ruit oute and extirpat all of that race." Breaking out of Eilean Mharnoch (Ellen's Isle) in Loch Katrine, where they were besieged, the MacGregors, doubtless recruiting as they went, carried fire and sword eastwards to Comrie and Fortingall and westwards to Loch Awe. Presently however, Robert, second son of Black Duncan, and Colin Campbell of Aberuchill drove them into the forest of Ben Buie in Argyll, then hunted them north of Rannoch, and scattered them.

By 1613 MacGregors of consequence were dead or had submitted to the Government ; those still at large were " bot unworthie poore miserable bodyis." Alasdair had no son ; and the Government had his brother's three lads in safe keeping. To extinguish their claims to Glenstrae, Glenorchy was allowed to enter Gregor, the eldest, as tenant of Glenstrae, their rights in which Glenorchy subsequently bought from the three brothers for £10,000. Duncan the Tutor surrendered, and was pardoned. A grandson of Ladasach, Robert Abrach (" of Lochaber ") had to purchase his pardon with six MacGregor heads. Robert and his kinsmen, however, did not keep permanently on the right side of the law. In 1621 they were in arms with " a nomber of the young broode " of the clan. Twelve years later the *Griogaraich* (MacGregors) were out again in half a dozen counties with the result that the laws against them were re-enacted ; Gilderoy of the ballad (*An Gille Ruadh*, the Red Lad) was hanged in 1636. Nevertheless the Government's purpose was substantially attained. Members of Clan Gregor took other names. Iain Dubh's boys became Murrays ;

Duncan the Tutor called himself Douglas ; Roro was a Gordon, Malcolm Oig of Clan Dougal Ciar, a Stewart, Brackley, a Graham, and so on, on occasion with their MacGregor name as an alternative (e.g. 1655, " Patrick Graham sumtyme McGregour "). To the ordinary members of the clan, among whom Gaelic patronymics would still have been in common use, the prohibition of the MacGregor surname may have been less significant than the other penalties imposed upon them. These were indeed grievous. That the clan survived at all was due largely to the " resetting " of individual MacGregors among other clans, in spite of the heavy fines thereby incurred, to a total of £115,000. The Laird of Grant, whose clan, like the MacGregors, claimed descent from Alpin, headed the list with nearly £27,000—an honourable pre-eminence. For, although there were various motives for befriending MacGregors, most widespread were " the promptings of common humanity, which make the records of the large sums collected from resetters of all classes throughout all the Highland counties the brightest page in the MacGregor history " (Audrey Cunningham, *The Loyal Clans*).

It is, therefore, remarkable that, when in 1644 Montrose raised King Charles I's standard in the Highlands, the MacGregors as a clan, in spite of further dispersion through " resetting," were in a position to seize this opportunity to earn their legal restoration by military service. No doubt their pride of race had continued to sustain them. Perhaps, too, the loose organisation, that had been a disadvantage in the past, was now a help. Through the clan's dispersion, administration must always have been in the hands of the branch chieftains, and when the clan was shattered, the branches could survive. We have seen that the clan's Name had not gone wholly out of mind ; and it has been suggested that in the branches the use of Gaelic patronymics would have been prevalent in any case. The historian of Clan Gregor says that Clan Dougal Ciar " were wont only to call themselves MacGregor if the father had the Christian name " ; in other instances they used the name of the branch, rendered phonetically by Scots writers as " McCoull chere." Similarly a member of the branch of Roro called himself, not MacGregor, but MacDhonnchaidh, " son of Duncan," after Duncan Beg, the founder of that branch. If these patronymics were deemed to comply with the law, the unity of those branches would thereby be preserved. The retention in the Highlands of the MacGregor " bairns " had further ensured that in 1644 there were still men in the Highlands who had been born MacGregors. By a later date the clan might have dissolved. Either the King's party or the party of the Covenant could have restored their Name, with their civil rights, to the clan in the event of victory, and to the Stuarts Clan Gregor owed no gratitude ; nevertheless for the King they drew their swords. For they wanted more than their Name and their civil rights ; they wanted Glenorchy and Glenlyon, the heritage, as their poets told them, of their forefathers. These they could get only at the expense of the Campbells ; and the Campbells were adversaries of the King.

Patrick Roy, second son of Iain Dubh, had succeeded his elder brother as Laird of MacGregor, which title the heads of the clan adopted, though illegally, after their loss of Glenstrae. Properties at the west end of Loch Rannoch, which he claimed from Menzies and, on refusal, forcibly occupied, gave him, as that remote district had given Ladasach and Alasdair, the rudiments of a clan " country," for here were settled cadets of Roro, the families of Dunan and Leiragan. In December 1644 the MacGregors joined Montrose to raid Argyll, fighting thereafter at Inverlochy and Kilsyth. With his fellow chiefs " Patrik McGregre of that Ilk " signed the Chiefs' Bond at Cill Chuimein (Fort Augustus) ; and from Montrose Patrick obtained, on condition of his clan's continued service, a guarantee that " whatsoever lands and possessions belonged justlie to the Laird of McGregor and his predecessors in Glenlyon, Rannoch, or Glenurchy" should be restored " when it shall please God to put an end to thes present troubles." In the meantime, however, the right of alien landlords to military service from their tenants remained inconsistent with the desire of Mac-Gregors to fight as a clan under their chief. When in 1651 Malcolm, son of Duncan the Tutor (and himself Tutor of James, son of Patrick Roy), was gathering his clan, Atholl and the Laird of Buchanan required the services of many of Malcolm's men, who were their dependants. Nevertheless Malcolm brought out two hundred of his people in the Rising under Glencairn, when MacGregor's " Hall " in the Isle of Loch Rannoch was a rendezvous for the royalist clans. It was perhaps during this period that the clan adopted their second motto, " E'en do and spare not " graven on the tombstone of Malcolm's son, Gregor, on Inchcailloch in Loch Lomond.

When " thes present troubles " came to an end, Clan Gregor's services were held to have cancelled " their former miscarriages." Their Name was restored to them, with the other privileges of loyal subjects (April 1661). King Charles II could have done no less ; he did nothing to implement the guarantee of Montrose to Patrick Roy. A hereditary territory in the legal possession of the chief would vastly have assisted the restoration of the clan. It may be that The MacGregor could show no right in law to the lands alleged to have belonged to his predecessors. At any rate Clan Gregor remained landless, and under these conditions apparently continued to maintain themselves illegally in Rannoch, since Menzies was excused responsibility for " the Clan Greigour in Rannoch." But later Lairds did not reside there. Malcolm the Tutor, his son Gregor, who succeeded James, son of Patrick Roy as Laird, and the next Laird, Gregor's cousin Archibald, all lived near Loch Lomond, on which Archibald purchased the estate of Craig Rostan. Their move southwards is likely to have been influenced by the fact that the territory of Clan Dougal Ciar provided here a clan " country " that was compact (being the upper western portions of their three glens), more ample than the properties which the MacGregors held in Rannoch, and comparable to Rannoch in security, though less remote. MacGregor of Glengyle, their chieftain, could probably muster some two hundred fighting men, for these glens must have been much more densely peopled than they are to-day. In Glen Arklet, fifty years later, through excessive sub-letting, one hundred and fifty families lived, however poorly, around Inversnaid. The Glengyle estate was in 1703 bought for the chieftain from the Duke of Montrose ; and two years later Clan Dougal Ciar's territory was rounded off when Rob Roy, Glengyle's uncle, acquired Craig Rostan from the Laird of Mac-Gregor. From the Lowlands this territory was accessible only by tracks through the Passes of Leny, Achray, Aberfoyle, and Balmaha ; and the whole district was unsuitable for " policing " by the regular troops who had replaced previous Governments' necessary reliance on neighbouring landlords. Inversnaid could indeed be reached by water from Dumbarton *via* the river Leven and Loch Lomond, for which reason the Government built a fort there to control the MacGregors. It seems, however, to have been incomplete in 1715, and in 1745 was captured by Glengyle.

Both Roro and Glengyle led their followers to support King James VII in 1689 ; too late to fight at Killie- crankie, MacGregors fought under Dundee's successor, Cannon, at Dunkeld. They fought in vain. The Revolution brought King William and Queen Mary to the throne ; and the penal statutes against the Mac- Gregors were re-imposed in 1693. The clan thus became again Nameless ; and the death of Archibald, the last representative of the House of Glenstrae, presently left them also Chiefless. Some of the principal MacGregor families, however, saw the offer of pensions to Highland chiefs by Queen Anne's Tory Government as a favourable opportunity to reconstitute the clan. Only to a chief would the Queen's pension be paid ; if official recog- nition of a MacGregor chief could be obtained, the clan would seem to have anticipated that the repeal of the penal laws against them would follow. On the under- standing that he would share the royal bounty with them, Roro, Glengyle, and Brackley with nine gentlemen of the clan in July 1714 declared Alexander MacGregor, or Drummond, of Balhaldie, as chief of Clan Gregor, the chiefship to continue hereditarily in his family.

This careful scheme to reconstitute Clan Gregor was frustrated. Balhaldie's claim to the chiefship was contested. His family were only junior cadets of Roro ; and while Roro, Glengyle, and Brackley had waived their claims in his favour, another candidate had been passed over, perhaps because, although a Jacobite, he was less active as such than Balhaldie. This was John MacGregor, or Murray, the representative of the family of Duncan Ladasach, and thereby, according to the historian of Clan Gregor, the representative of the House of Gregor McAne, senior to Brackley in that House and also to Roro and Glengyle in the clan. This latter seniority was perhaps not universally accepted. John MacGregor did not " come out " in 1715. Subsequently, however, he bought an estate in Balquhidder, from which he became known as MacGregor of Glencarnaig (or Glencarnoch). This was significant, for probably only Clan Dougal Ciar could now put a considerable body of clansmen in the field. Since 1633, for example, Roro held merely the Mains of Roro, and that under a wadset, or mortgage. In other areas MacGregors were more intermingled with other clans than they were in Clan Dougal Ciar's, and were apt to prefer living on good terms with their neighbours to fighting them for the sake of the exiled Stuarts. The clan's Name had been banned for over twenty years ; young " MacGregors " had never borne that Name. Another formidable obstacle still hampered Clan Gregor. By law military service was due to feudal superiors, not to clan chiefs, as such. It is ironical to reflect that the abolition of heritable jurisdictions, actually effected in 1747, would at an earlier date have assisted the reconstitution of Clan Gregor by removing this obligation, which among them practically only Clan Dougal Ciar seem to have been able to ignore. Under these circumstances any scheme for the reconstitution of the clan could go forward hopefully only under conditions of peace, and with a Government in power which was at least not actively anti-Jacobite. In August, however, Qneen Anne died. With the accession of King George I the payment of pensions to Highland chiefs ceased ; and with this any hope of the official recognition of a chief of Clan Gregor perished. Thirteen months later began the Rising of 1715.

Those MacGregors who joined the Earl of Mar, possibly on his promise of the repeal of the penal statutes against them, were chiefly Clan Dougal Ciar under Gregor Glun Dubh (" Black Knee ") of Glengyle, his uncle, Rob Roy, and Balhaldie. Of these, Rob Roy was probably the most influential. He was the only leading member of the clan to fight for King James VIII at Glenshiel in 1719; but in 1715 he seems to have been less interested in the Jacobite cause than in a private war with the Duke of Montrose, who had acquired the Menteith and Buchanan estates. Montrose's tenants were forced to buy immunity from the MacGregors' depredations by paying " black-mail " to Rob Roy. His exploits have made him possibly the best known of all Highlanders. In his own day they served his clan ill by perpetuating the reputation that " plunder and Booty is their Bussiness." Such reputation, it must be admitted, under the conditions imposed upon them while their Name was proscribed, they had done enough to earn. Hence MacGregors were excluded from the Pardon granted in 1717.

Rob Roy kept John MacGregor Murray out of Glencarnaig for five years, and thus out of the only locality where he could win significant support. Nevertheless by 1745 Robert, his son and heir, was able to bring to Prince Charles Edward's army a contingent larger than that of Glengyle. Although many MacGregors seem to have received him as their chief, he accepted the rank of Lieutenant-Colonel in the clan regiment under Glengyle. Glun Dubh, however, was elderly; and it was Glencarnaig who commanded the regiment at Prestonpans (where they won honour) and on the march to Derby. William of Balhaldie, Alexander's son and successor, was not in Scotland in 1745.

The penal statutes against the MacGregors were not repealed until November 1774, when it became lawful for the *Griogaraich* again to bear their Name. Thereupon a gathering of over eight hundred clansmen acknowledged as their chief John Murray of Lanrick, a nephew of Glencarnaig of the Forty-Five. In 1795 the Lord Lyon King of Arms confirmed to Sir John Murray (now a Baronet) the chief arms of Clan Gregor, and he became MacGregor of MacGregor.   In 1798 he bought the estate of Edinchip, near Lochearnhead, in Perthshire, which has remained the seat of the chiefs of Clan Gregor. The present chief, Lt.-Col. Sir Gregor MacGregor of MacGregor, sixth Baronet, was born in 1925. His heir is his elder son, Malcolm Gregor Charles, born 1959.

Pipe Music of Clan Gregor

A gifted MacGregor family of Glenlyon called the Clann an Sgeulaiche, or Race of the Story-teller, was noted for its succession of musicians, bards, and sennachies. The pipers were pipers to their chiefs until well into the seventeenth century. In the eighteenth century members were pipers to Rob Roy, Simon Lord Lovat, Menzies of Menzies, the Duke of Atholl, the Earl of Breadalbane, the Highland Society of London, and Prince Charles Edward himself. From 1781 to 1813 at least seventeen of the family competed in the Highland Society's Edinburgh competitions commenced in 1781. Twelve were first prize winners, and of these all probably were descendants of a single man, John MacGregor (1708-1789). This John joined the Prince at Glenfinnan and served him as piper and personal attendant throughout the campaign. He was wounded at Culloden, but managed to get home and for the rest of his life was piper to Col. Campbell of Glenlyon. His four piper sons and eight grandsons were all eminent. His last known prize-winning descendant was piper to Menzies and died in 1921.

Always excepting the MacCrimmons, the Clann an Sgeulaiche seems to have been the most distinguished piping family *of which we have any record*. It is said that, at one time, they had a piping school at Drumcharry in Glenlyon and used to send their best pupil for a year to Skye to the MacCrimmons.

We do not know whether this galaxy of playing talent composed any of the many fine piobaireachds which have come down to us without authors' names. The only tune traditionally ascribed to a member of the family (a somewhat shadowy Duncan Mor) is *Ruaig Ghlinn Fraoin* (The Rout of Glenfruin) to which the Campbell Canntaireachd MS. (*c.* 1790) gives the alternative name of " MacGrigor's March." It is one of the finest in existence.

Another MacGregor piobaireachd, also much esteemed nowadays, but of unknown authorship, is The MacGregors' Salute or Gathering. The author of *Albyn's Anthology*, Alexander Campbell, was given it in cann-taireachd, syllabic notation, in 1815 by Capt. Neil MacLeod of Gesto in Skye. With some trouble he was able to translate and extract from it an air for Sir Walter Scott's song, The MacGregors' Gathering, which nowadays is sung to a different air. Campbell's original air will be found in the second volume of *Albyn's Anthology* (1818).

A third piobaireachd is one of several names and several versions. It is listed as a possible Fraser tune on p. 29 of *The Clan Fraser of Lovat* by C. I. Fraser of Reelig (1952). But the oldest record, The Campbell Canntaireachd, calls it " MacGrigor's Gathering," and for that reason it may be a MacGregor tune, and also because most of the other names, Castle Menzies, Menzie of that Ilk, Piobaireachd Uaimh, Fraser's Lament and Fraser's Salute could be links with the Clann an Sgeulaiche. More than one of that family were pipers to Menzies at Weem, and Ewen MacGregor, Simon Lord Lovat's piper, and by repute a great player, was also a member of it.

A well-known slow air, MacGregor of Ruaro, to which a song of that name is sung, can be included in the Clan Pipe Music. It is sometimes called MacGregor's Lament, and appears to be ancient.

ARCHIBALD CAMPBELL OF KILBERRY

Clan Gregor Names

(From *Clans, Septs, and Regiments of the Scottish Highlands*, By Frank Adam. Seventh Edition, revised by Sir Thomas Innes of Learney, Lord Lyon King of Arms.)

Black	Grierson	Maccrouther	MacNie
Caird	Grigor	Macgrewar	MacNish
Comrie	Gruer	Macgrowther	MacPeter
Dochart	King	Macgruder	MacPetrie
Fletcher	Leckie	Macgruther	Malloch
Gregor	Lecky	Macilduy	Neish
Gregorson	MacAdam	MacLeister	Nish
Gregory	Macara	MacLiver	Peter
Greig	Macaree	MacNee	White
Grewar	MacChoiter	MacNeish	Whyte
Grier	MacConachie		

Acknowledgement

I am deeply indebted to Dr. I. F. Grant and the late Major C. I. Fraser of Reelig, sometime Albany Herald, who read the typescript of this book and greatly improved it by their suggestions ; to Mr. Archibald Campbell of Kilberry, who supplied the invaluable Note on Pipe Music ; and to the late Miss Margaret O. MacDougall, for information on the Tartans.
For the MacGregor genealogy, see also Burke's *Peerage*, 1970.